The Best Mud Pie

Written by Lin Quinn
Illustrated by Ronnie Rooney

SCHOLASTIC INC.

New York   Toronto   London   Auckland   Sydney
Mexico City   New Delhi   Hong Kong   Buenos Aires

Tom, for you Babe—I Love You!
— L.Q.

To Aodhan, Tommy, Katie, and Peter
Love, your auntie Ronnie

Reading Consultant
Katharine A. Kane
Education Consultant
(Retired, San Diego County Office of Education and San Diego State University)

ISBN 0-516-24128-1

12 11 10 9 8 7 6   4 5 6 7/0

Printed in the U.S.A.   10

First Scholastic printing, February 2002

the great chef.

Here are my bowls and spoons.

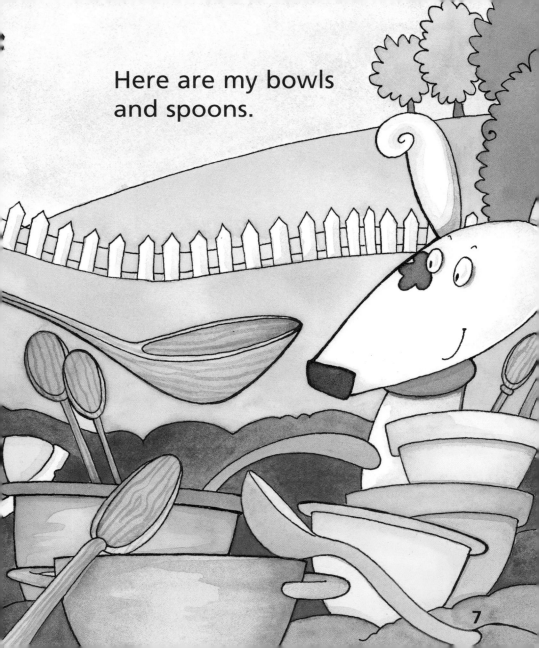

Here are my
pots and pans.

9

My mud pies are the best!

Put sandy dirt and
sticky dirt in a bowl.

Mix with a spoon.

Add water—not too much.

Put small pinecones and shiny rocks in a pot.

19

Mix in broken sticks.

Add water.
Oh dear—too much!

Pat in a pan.
Top with leaves.

Serve mud pie with a smile.

Everyone wants my recipe,

29

but it's a family secret. Shhh!

Word List (56 words)

a	family	pans	shhh
add	great	pat	shiny
am	here	pie	small
and	I	pies	smile
are	in	pinecones	spoon
best	it's	pot	spoons
bowl	leaves	pots	sticks
bowls	mix	put	sticky
broken	much	recipe	the
but	mud	Roberto	too
chef	my	rocks	top
dear	not	sandy	wants
dirt	oh	secret	water
everyone	pan	serve	with

About the Author

Lin Quinn loves to get messy, whether it's with mud or her paints. This is her first book, but she promises it won't be her last! She continues to write and paint in her home in southern California, where she lives with her husband, Tom, three teenagers, Rian, Sean, and Meghan, two cats, and a large German shepherd. Life is messy at Lin's house, but always full of love.

About the Illustrator

Ronnie Rooney was born and raised in Massachusetts. She attended the University of Massachusetts in Amherst, and received her M.F.A. in illustration at Savannah College of Art and Design in Savannah, Georgia. When Ronnie isn't illustrating greeting cards or children's books, she loves to swim, run, and eat chocolate chip cookie dough. (But not all at the same time!) She lives in Plymouth, Massachusetts.